THIS BOOK BELONGS TO...

Name:	Age:

Favourite player:

2020/2021

My Predictions...   Actual...

The Whites' final position:

The Whites' top scorer:

Premier League winners:

Premier League top scorer:

FA Cup winners:

EFL Cup winners:

Contributors: Peter Rogers

A TWOCAN PUBLICATION

©2020. Published by twocan under licence from Leeds United FC.

ISBN 978-1-913362-30-0

£9

ILLAN 1 MESLIER

POSITION: Goalkeeper   **DOB:** 02/03/2000
COUNTRY: France

French goalkeeper Illan Meslier agreed a permanent switch to Leeds United in the summer of 2020 having spent the Championship title-winning season on loan at Elland Road from Lorient.

The giant French under-20 international made his Whites' debut in the club's FA Cup third-round tie away to Arsenal and went on to record seven clean sheets in his ten Championship outings.

2 LUKE AYLING

POSITION: Defender   **DOB:** 25/08/1991
COUNTRY: England

Right-back Luke Ayling has amassed over 150 appearances for Leeds United following a 2016 move from Bristol City.

The popular defender was again a regular face in Marcelo Bielsa's starting line-up in 2019/20, making 37 appearances in the club's promotion-winning campaign and also netting the Whites' Goal of the Season with a stunning volley in the 2-0 home win over Huddersfield Town in March 2020.

KALVIN *Phillips*

SOCCER SKILLS

Great goalkeepers are an essential ingredient for successful teams in today's game. They have to excel in all areas of the art of 'keeping and Kiko Casilla is a great 'keeper that lives up to these expectations.

DISTRIBUTION
THE BASICS OF GOOD THROWING TECHNIQUE

OVERARM THROW

This is best for covering long distances. The body should be in line with the direction of the throw with the weight on the back foot. The ball should be brought forward in a bowling action with the arm straight.

JAVELIN THROW

This throw is made quickly with a low trajectory. The arm is bent for this throw, the ball is held beside the head and the body is in line with the direction of the throw. The arm is brought forward in a pushing movement with the ball being released at the top.

UNDERARM THROW

The ball is released from a crouching position, with a smooth underarm swing.

Throws do not usually travel as far as kicks but the greater speed and accuracy of throwing can make up for the lack of distance and will help the team retain possession. A player receiving a throw must be able to control it early.

Work hard at distribution and the benefits of this will be seen whenever you are in possession during a match.

EXERCISE ONE

Grab a friend and throw the ball to each other using the various throwing techniques at various distances apart.

EXERCISE TWO

The goalkeeper with the ball uses the various throws to knock another ball off a marker.

EXERCISE THREE

The goalkeepers try to throw the ball through the markers using various throwing techniques.

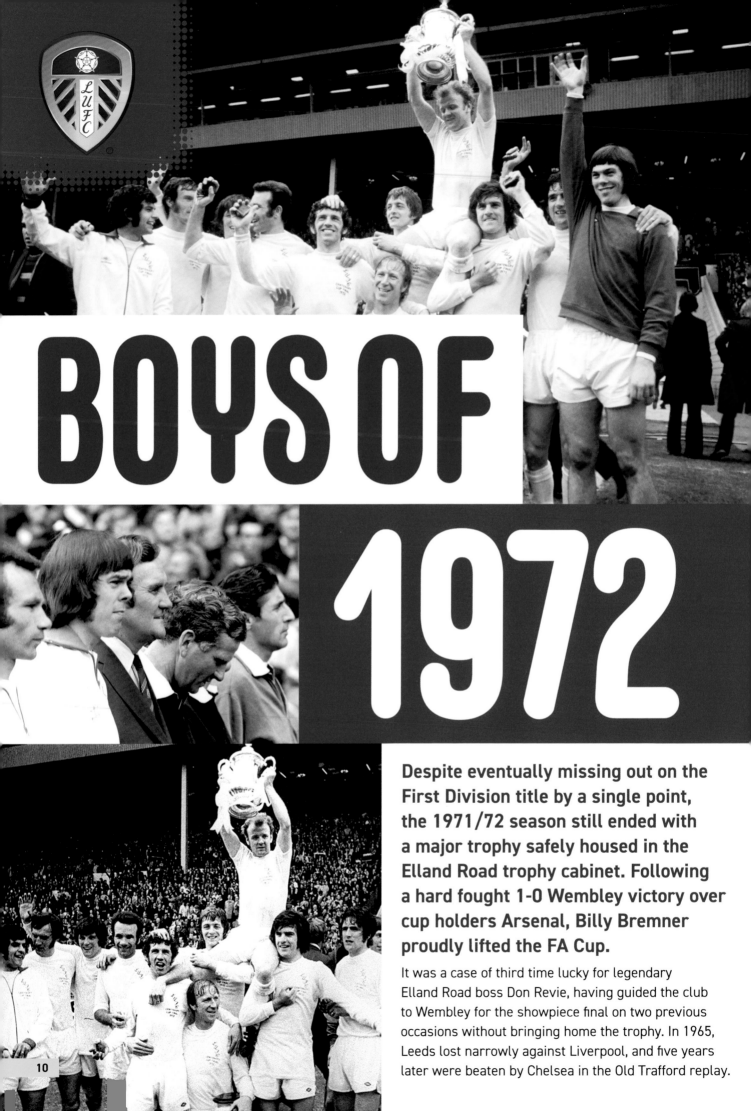

BOYS OF 1972

Despite eventually missing out on the First Division title by a single point, the 1971/72 season still ended with a major trophy safely housed in the Elland Road trophy cabinet. Following a hard fought 1-0 Wembley victory over cup holders Arsenal, Billy Bremner proudly lifted the FA Cup.

It was a case of third time lucky for legendary Elland Road boss Don Revie, having guided the club to Wembley for the showpiece final on two previous occasions without bringing home the trophy. In 1965, Leeds lost narrowly against Liverpool, and five years later were beaten by Chelsea in the Old Trafford replay.

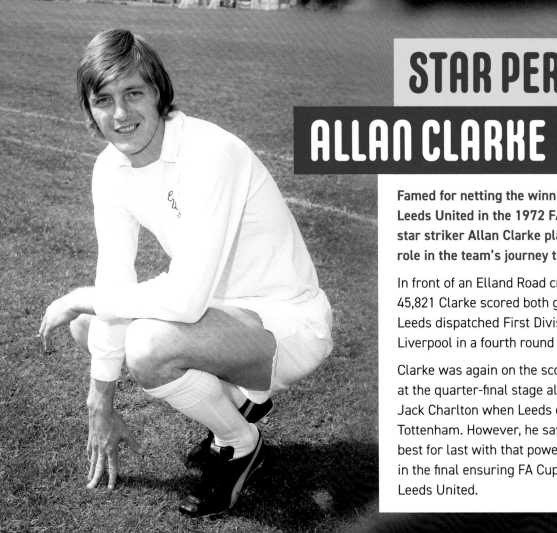

STAR PERFORMER
ALLAN CLARKE

Famed for netting the winning goal for Leeds United in the 1972 FA Cup final, star striker Allan Clarke played a vital role in the team's journey to Wembley.

In front of an Elland Road crowd of 45,821 Clarke scored both goals as Leeds dispatched First Division rivals Liverpool in a fourth round replay.

Clarke was again on the scoresheet at the quarter-final stage along with Jack Charlton when Leeds edged past Tottenham. However, he saved his best for last with that powerful header in the final ensuring FA Cup glory for Leeds United.

Embroiled in a four-way battle for the title with Derby County, Liverpool and Manchester City - Leeds began their pursuit of FA Cup success with a routine 4-1 third-round defeat of Third Division Bristol Rovers.

The fourth round presented Revie's men with the chance of some cup revenge for the final defeat of 1965 when they were paired with Liverpool. Following a goalless draw at Anfield, Leeds progressed to round five with a 2-0 win in the Elland Road replay.

A 2-0 win away against Second Division Cardiff City preceded a hard-fought quarter-final victory at home to Tottenham Hotspur. A comfortable 3-0 semi-final triumph over Birmingham City at Hillsborough then lined up a treasured place in the final against the Gunners.

Striker Allan Clarke became Leeds' cup final hero, when he headed home a Mick Jones cross eight minutes into the second half for the game's only goal. The FA Cup was heading to Leeds.

TEAM 2020/21

ADAM FORSHAW 4

POSITION: Midfielder   **DOB:** 08/10/1991
COUNTRY: England

Liverpool-born midfielder Adam Forshaw joined the Whites from Middlesbrough during the 2018 January transfer window.

After some impressive performances in 2018/19, Forshaw continued his good form in Leeds' excellent start to their 2019/20 title success. Sadly, after featuring in seven Championship matches at the start of the season, Forshaw suffered a hip injury which required surgery and ruled him out for the remainder of the campaign.

5 ROBIN KOCH

POSITION: Defender   **DOB:** 17/07/1996
COUNTRY: Spain

Leeds United added highly-rated central-defender Robin Koch to their ranks after securing the German's services on a four-year deal from Bundesliga club SC Freiburg.

The former Eintracht Trier and Kaiserslautern defender has gained a glowing reputation as a top quality ball playing centre-back and had won two full German caps ahead of his transfer to Elland Road.

LIAM 6 COOPER

POSITION: Defender **DOB:** 30/08/1991
COUNTRY: Scotland

Captain Liam Cooper formed a reliable partnership with Ben White as Leeds recorded 22 clean sheets en route to the Championship title last season.

A £600,000 recruit from Chesterfield in 2014, Cooper is closing in on 200 appearances for the club. The Scottish international netted the equaliser away at Brentford in February 2020 and was also on target in the 5-0 rout of Stoke City in July as Leeds closed in on promotion.

GOAL
OF THE SEASON

LUKE AYLING

V HUDDERSFIELD TOWN

7 MARCH 2020

There were certainly some cracking strikes among the 77 Championship goals netted by Leeds United en route to landing the 2019/20 Sky Bet Championship title. However, only one goal can be crowned Goal of the Season and that honour went to Luke Ayling for his fantastic volley against Huddersfield Town.

There were just three minutes on the clock of a vital West Yorkshire derby against the Terriers at Elland Road on Saturday 7 March 2020 when Ayling smashed a volley in off the crossbar to give the Whites an early lead.

The goal was Ayling's fourth goal of the campaign, with the attacking full-back also having been on target a week earlier in the 4-0 victory away at Hull City. His other strikes came in the 1-0 Elland Road victory over Bristol City and also in the never-to-be-forgotten 5-4 thriller with Birmingham City at St Andrew's in December 2019.

In front of a derby-day crowd of 36,514, Leeds took control when Pablo Hernandez fed the ball to Jack Harrison wide on the left and his deep cross was met by the on-rushing Ayling with a ferocious volley which left visiting 'keeper Jonas Lossl helpless as the stadium erupted to salute the full-back's wonder-strike.

The goal was both spectacular and important in equal measure as it paved the way for another three points in the Whites' promotion push. Patrick Bamford wrapped up the win with a close-range finish after Lossl could only tip Ben White's header into his path. The win gave Leeds the local bragging rights and moved them seven points clear of third-placed Fulham.

Ironically this game was Leeds' final fixture before the coronavirus lockdown, which suspended football before the season was later concluded with matches played behind closed doors. What a travesty it would have been if Ayling's goal had not been witnessed by a full house at Elland Road. His timing really was just perfect!

Challenge your favourite grown-up and find out which of you is the biggest Premier League brain!

ADULTS

Who is the captain of Wolverhampton Wanderers?

1 ANSWER

Can you name the four Premier League clubs that reached the 2019/20 FA Cup semi-finals?

2 ANSWER

At which club did Chelsea boss Frank Lampard begin his managerial career?

3 ANSWER

Who is the oldest manager in the Premier League?

4 ANSWER

At which club did Southampton's star striker Danny Ings begin his career?

5 ANSWER

From which club did Manchester United sign Bruno Fernandes?

6 ANSWER

At which club did Newcastle manager Steve Bruce begin his playing career?

7 ANSWER

How many clubs from the north west have won the Premier League title?

8 ANSWER

Which was the first London club to win the Premier League?

9 ANSWER

Which Premier League manager is also his club's record goalscorer?

10 ANSWER

16

V KIDS

The adults' questions are on the left page and the kids' questions are on the right page.

ANSWERS ON PAGE 62

Which team began the 2020/21 Premier League season as defending champions for the first time?

1

What nationality is Chelsea striker Timo Werner?

2

How many Premier League clubs have the title 'United' in their name?

3

Who plays their home games at Molineux?

4

Which Premier League ground has the largest capacity?

5

Which current Premier League club won last season's League Cup?

6

What is Everton's nickname?

7

Can you name the club that play their home matches at St James' Park?

8

Who is the manager of Leicester City?

9

What nationality is Tottenham Hotspur manager, Jose Mourinho?

10

Fill the page with your footy goals and dreams, no matter how big or small, and then start working on how to accomplish them!

We've started you off...

1. Visit Elland Road

2. Complete 50 keepy-uppies

FOOTY BUCKET LIST

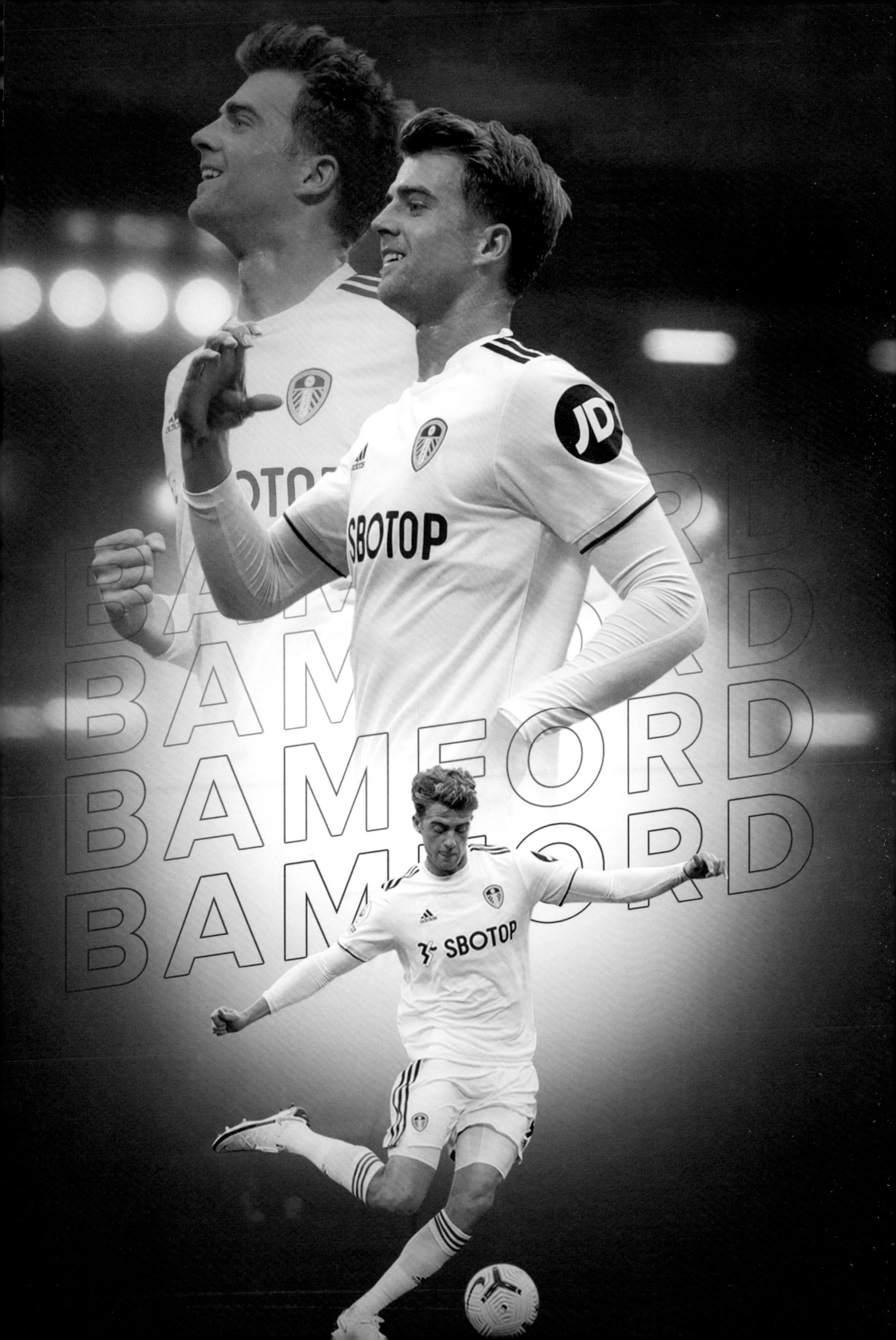
BAMFORD
BAMFORD
BAMFORD
BAMFORD
BAMFORD
SBOTOP
SBOTOP

6

7

WHO

Can you figure out the identity of all these Leeds United stars?

ARE YER?

8

9

10

ANSWERS ON PAGE 62

IAN 7
POVEDA

POSITION: Midfielder   **DOB:** 09/02/2000
COUNTRY: England

An England under-20 international, winger Ian Poveda joined the Whites during the 2020 January transfer window from Manchester City.

A tricky wide-man with an eye for goal, Poveda agreed a four-and-a-half year deal at Elland Road. He made his Leeds United debut against Cardiff City on 21 June and also featured in victories over Fulham, Derby County and Charlton Athletic.

PATRICK 9
BAMFORD

POSITION: Striker   **DOB:** 05/09/1993
COUNTRY: England

Patrick Bamford topped the Elland Road scoring charts with 16 goals in 2019/20 as Leeds United secured the Championship title and promotion to the Premier League.

Barmford's 16-goal haul last season included double strikes against Wigan Athletic, Cardiff City and Millwall. Signed from Middlesbrough in July 2018, the ace marksman will be relishing the opportunity of pitting his wits against Premier League defenders in 2020/21.

10 EZGJAN ALIOSKI

POSITION: Defender   **DOB:** 12/02/1992
COUNTRY: Macedonia

Fully committed to the Leeds United cause, Ezgjan Alioski's determined and all-action approach to games has seen him become a firm favourite with the Elland Road faithful.

He has the ability to play at left-back or in a more advanced role. The 2019/20 Championship title-winning campaign saw him make 39 appearances and chip in with five vital goals too.

23

Having suffered Play-Off heartbreak at the end of the 2018/19 season, Marcelo Bielsa's men responded in perfect style in 2019/20 by landing the Sky Bet Championship title and ending the club's 16-year absence from the Premier League.

When Leeds United kicked off the season away at Bristol City on Sunday 4 August 2019, no-one could ever have anticipated that the Whites would still be battling away for promotion almost 12 months later! However, this was no ordinary season and it will certainly go down as one of the most eventful and historic in the club's rich history.

In an action-packed campaign that certainly became the longest-running Leeds United season, not even the coronavirus pandemic could stop Bielsa's boys from marching on to Premier League promotion.

The Whites had clearly put their Play-Off frustrations firmly behind them when the season got underway at Ashton Gate with goals from Pablo Hernandez, Patrick Bamford and Jack Harrison securing a 3-1 win over Bristol City and put a marker down that once again Leeds United meant business.

In a sensational start to the season, the team really hit the ground running and took 16 points from the first 18 available. A vital 1-0 Elland Road victory over fellow promotion hopefuls West Bromwich Albion also saw October off to a winning start. Tyler Roberts and Jack Harrison were on target in the opening match of November when Leeds defeated Queens Park Rangers 2-0 at home, and that victory triggered a run of seven straight Championship wins with the Whites extending their lead at the top of the table.

The calendar year of 2019 ended in dramatic style with an incredible 5-4 victory away against Birmingham City. Trailing 4-3 with seven minutes to play, Leeds mounted an outstanding finale to take all three points If ever there was a match that typified the never-say-die attitude of Biesla's team, then this surely was it.

January 2020 ended with a crucial home win over Millwall and the Whites went on to maintain top spot with another five Championship victories before football was halted in March 2020 with nine league matches remaining.

With the country in lockdown due to the coronavirus pandemic, Bielsa and his staff kept the players fit and ready for a return to action while also maintaining the group's burning desire to get the season completed and achieve their Premier League dream.

Project Restart saw the Whites finally back in action, albeit with no crowds, on 21 June. The restarted season began with a 2-0 defeat away against Play-Off chasing Cardiff City, but was swiftly followed by a 3-0 win over Fulham at an eerily quiet Elland Road.

Leeds won seven of their final nine games despite playing without the backing of their passionate supporters inside the stadiums. That run of form proved enough to see the team promoted as champions with two games to spare. Leeds United were Championship title winners and heading back to the Premier League!

After battling away for precious points throughout the 2019/20 season, Leeds United reaped the rewards of their sustained efforts in July 2020 as the promotion dream became reality.

Hard-fought 1-0 victories away at Swansea City and at home against Barnsley left Marcelo Bielsa's team within touching distance of both promotion and the Championship title. In fact, just 24 hours after the Whites had defeated Yorkshire rivals Barnsley at Elland Road, they were able to celebrate promotion to the Premier League without even having to kick a ball!

Despite Leeds not being in action, their promotion was still secured by events in West Yorkshire. On Friday 17 July, promotion-rivals West Bromwich Albion suffered a 2-1 defeat away against Huddersfield Town and that result meant only Brentford could overtake the table-topping Whites and therefore promotion to the Premier League was assured.

Members of the squad had assembled at Elland Road to watch the match and made an appearance from the windows of the ground to celebrate with supporters who had made their way to the stadium for this special moment.

With the team's next fixture scheduled for Sunday 19 July at Derby County, the city of Leeds certainly partied on the Saturday, with fans knowing their 16-year wait to see their heroes back in the top flight was over. However, Saturday, 18 July saw everyone associated with Leeds United having cause for a double celebration. Brentford suffered a 1-0 defeat away against Stoke City which in turn guaranteed Leeds United the Championship title with two games to play.

With the title and promotion in the bag, Leeds played their final away match of the season at Derby County where the Rams players provided a guard of honour to welcome the champions onto the pitch. A much-changed line-up marked the club's promotion in style by coming from behind to record a 3-1 win before celebrating at the end of the game with champagne and the traditional 'We're going up!' banners.

The season finally reached its conclusion on Wednesday 22 July when Leeds turned on the style to defeat Charlton Athletic 4-0 before being presented with the Championship trophy. Despite the match sadly taking place behind closed doors, it did not prevent fans flocking to the stadium to salute their title-winning heroes.

Take our quick-fire personality test to see where Marcelo Bielsa would utilise your skills in the Whites' line-up...

WHICH FOOTBALLER ARE YOU?

1. What is your favourite activity at the park?

a. Leaping around

b. Practicing my heading

c. Lots of non-stop running

d. Scoring goals

2. What is your biggest strength?

a. My height

b. My strength

c. My stamina

d. My speed

3. Which would you rather win?

a. A game of catch

b. A weight lifting contest

c. A long distance run

d. A sprint race

4. You score a goal! How do you celebrate?

a. I turn and punch the air

b. I clench my fist in delight

c. I high-five a teammate

d. I slide on my knees

5. How would the opposition describe you?

a. Hard to beat

b. Determined to succeed

c. All-action

d. Lethal in front of goal

6. What's your favourite move?

a. Springing high to catch under pressure

b. A sliding tackle

c. Playing the perfect through ball

d. Spinning away from my marker

7. What is the key to winning a game?

a. Keeping a clean sheet

b. Winning your individual battles

c. Maintaining possession

d. Taking chances that come your way

8. What is your favourite number?

a. One

b. Five

c. Seven

d. Nine

9. How would you describe your style of play?

a. Disciplined

b. Fully committed

c. Relentless

d. Technically gifted

10. What do your teammates call you?

a. Secure

b. Reliable

c. Energetic

d. Mr/Miss goals

MOSTLY As

You would clearly be a safe pair of hands in goal. Watch out Kiko Casilla, there's competition here for the No1 shirt!

MOSTLY Bs

Sounds like you are a young Luke Ayling in the making - there could well be a role for you in the Leeds back four...

MOSTLY Cs

You could comfortably take your place in the heart of midfield and help make things tick at Elland Road. Move over Kalvin Phillips!

MOSTLY Ds

Looks like we have a budding Patrick Bamford on our hands! Who do you fancy partnering in attack?

TYLER 11
ROBERTS

POSITION: Striker   **DOB:** 12/01/1999
COUNTRY: England

An exciting attack-minded player, Tyler Roberts can play anywhere across the front line where his pace and eye for goal make him a real threat for defenders.

Signed from West Bromwich Albion in January 2018, Roberts has already been capped as a full international by Wales. He netted four Championship goals for Leeds in 2019/20 including a brace in the 4-0 victory away against Hull City in February 2020.

14 DIEGO LLORENTE

POSITION: Defender   **DOB:** 16/08/1993
COUNTRY: Spain

Spanish International defender Diego Llorente arrived at Elland Road in September 2020 on a four-year deal from La Liga outfit Real Sociedad.

Llorente started his career at Real Madrid, making his Bernabeu debut against Osasuna in June 2013. After spells with Rayo Vallecano and Malaga, he made the permanent switch to Sociedad in June 2017, where he made 88 appearances for the club over the last three seasons, scoring eight goals.

KIKO 13 CASILLA

POSITION: Goalkeeper   **DOB:** 02/10/1986
COUNTRY: Spain

Triple Champions League winner, Kiko Casilla joined Leeds United from Real Madrid in January 2019.

After making his debut in a 2-1 at Rotherham, the goalkeeper's arrival at Elland Road has certainly brought vast experience and knowhow to the Leeds backline. He made 36 appearances in last season's title-winning campaign, when his presence provided great assurance to those in front of him.

15 STUART DALLAS

POSITION: Defender   **DOB:** 19/04/1991
COUNTRY: Northern Ireland

Ever-present in all bar one game of the Whites' 2019/20 promotion-winning campaign, defender Stuart Dallas was voted the Players' Player of the Season at the end of an historic campaign at Elland Road.

An experienced Northern Ireland international, Dallas joined Leeds United from Brentford in the summer of 2015 and is now closing in on 200 appearances for the club.

BOYS OF 1974

Leeds United landed the First Division title for the second time in the space of six seasons when they were crowned league champions in 1973/74.

The club first won the Division One title in 1967/68 and under the masterful management of Don Revie, the Whites ended in the top three places in each of the following four seasons before then securing top spot once again.

The team made a flying start to the campaign, winning their opening seven league games. After drawing 0-0 with Manchester United, Revie's men were soon back

STAR PERFORMER
MICK JONES

Centre-forward Mick Jones was signed from Sheffield United back in September 1967 for a fee of £100,000. He went on to score 77 league goals in 220 appearances for Leeds United and was the leading marksman with 17 goals in the 1973/74 title-winning campaign.

Jones was on target in the opening day 3-1 win over Everton at Elland Road and formed a formidable striker partnership with Allan Clarke as Leeds United powered their way to the top of the table.

His 17-goal season included a brace in the 4-1 victory over West Ham United at Elland Road in November 1973 and he was also on target during the 2-0 win away against Manchester United in February 1974.

to their winning ways and at the turn of the year, they remained unbeaten in the league and topped the table with an eight-point cushion over second-placed Liverpool.

It was not until 23 February that Leeds suffered their first league defeat - going down 3-2 away against Stoke City. After overcoming a surprise run of three straight defeats in March, Leeds returned to form with a crucial 2-0 win at home against Derby County and then pressed on to secure the title. They ended the campaign with wins away against Sheffield United and Queens Park Rangers plus an excellent 3-2 Elland Road victory over Ipswich Town.

Having suffered just four league defeats all season, Leeds ended the season as champions with a 62-point return, five points ahead of runners-up Liverpool. It was at the end of this triumphant season that the club's greatest ever manager, Don Revie, left Elland Road to take up the challenge of managing the England national team.

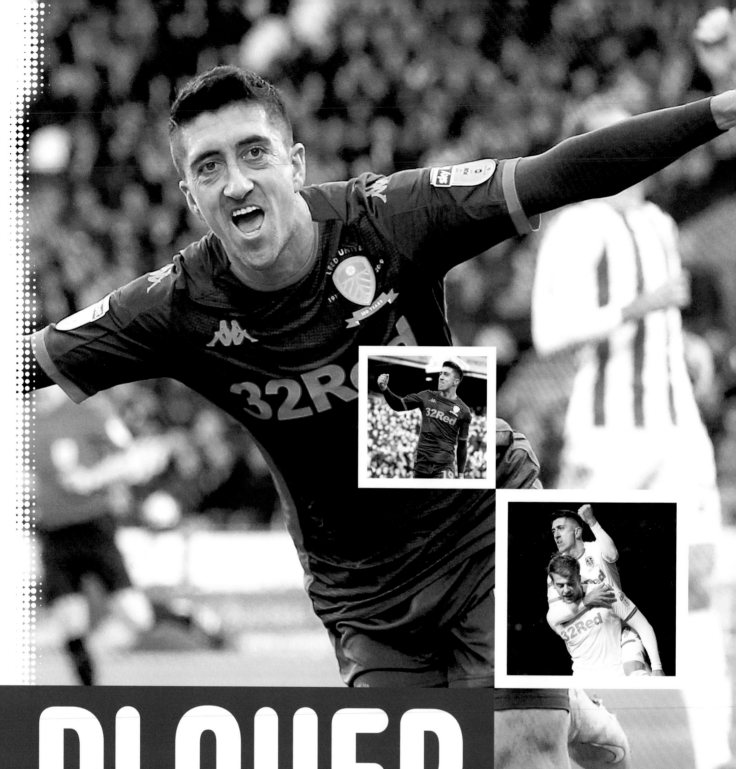

PLAYER
OF THE SEASON

PABLO HERNANDEZ

Pablo Hernandez etched his name further into Elland Road folklore when he was voted the Whites' Player of the Season for 2019/20. The skilful Spaniard took the award for the third consecutive season and became the first player in the club's history to achieve that feat.

In what was a hugely memorable campaign for Leeds United, who sealed a return to the Premier League by winning the Sky Bet Championship title, there were many contenders for the Player of the Season accolade. However, after playing a crucial role with a string of outstanding performances and vital goals, the fans once again gave Hernandez their votes and seal of approval as the top performer at Elland Road.

Fittingly for such an historic season, it was Hernandez who set the ball rolling by netting the Whites' first goal of the campaign, setting Marcelo Bielsa's men on their way to a 3-1 away against Bristol City on the opening weekend of the season.

Throughout the season, Hernandez made 36 appearances, scored nine goals and also contributed nine assists as Leeds marched to the top of the Championship table and on to promotion. The Elland Road faithful were given an early Christmas present with the news in November 2019 that their star man had agreed a contract extension which will keep him with the club until 2022.

Hernandez netted an important match-winning goal against Reading in February, but it was his dramatic last-minute strike away against his former club, Swansea City, which left Leeds United within touching distance of both promotion and the title.

YOUNG PLAYER OF THE SEASON
BEN WHITE

The club's Young Player of the Year award for 2019/20 went to ever-present defender Ben White. The central-defender, who spent the 2019/20 campaign at Elland Road after joining the club on a season-long loan deal from Brighton & Hove Albion, enjoyed a highly-impressive season and played a vital role in the team's 22 clean sheets en route to the Championship title.

White capped off a memorable loan spell when he netted his first goal for the club on his final appearance when Leeds ended the season with a 4-0 victory over Charlton Athletic.

"I came here not thinking I was going to be a massive part of the team and I've come here and played every single game which I didn't think was going to happen," said White after winning the award. "I'm so grateful for what has happened this year" he added.

HELDER **17** COSTA

POSITION: Midfielder **DOB:** 12/01/1994
COUNTRY: Portugal

After spending the 2019/20 season on loan at Elland Road from Wolverhampton Wanderers, flying winger Helder Costa completed a permanent transfer to Leeds United in July 2020 following the club's promotion to the Premier League.

A full Portuguese international, Costa made 43 appearances in the Whites' title success last season and netted four league goals including the opening strike in the incredible 5-4 win away to Birmingham City.

18 RAPHINHA

POSITION: Winger **DOB:** 14/12/1996
COUNTRY: Brazil

The 23-year-old Brazilian winger joined the Whites on a four-year deal from Ligue 1 side Rennes. He featured 30 times for the French outfit last season, scoring seven goals and providing five assists, with Rennes finishing third and qualifying for the UEFA Champions League.

On his last appearance for the club this season, he scored, and left the club at the top of the table. Raphinha also has experience of European competition, having appeared in the UEFA Europa League with Vitória, Sporting CP and Rennes.

PABLO 19 HERNANDEZ

POSITION: Midfielder **DOB:** 11/04/85
COUNTRY: Spain

Pablo Hernandez enjoyed another sensational season at Elland Road in 2019/20 and ended the campaign with the club's Player of the Season award for the third consecutive season.

A real creative spark in the Whites' midfield, Hernandez topped the assists chart by creating nine goals and also netting nine goals himself as Leeds won the Championship title. The skilful Spaniard will be keen to showcase his talents at Premier League level in 2020/21.

20 RODRIGO MORENO MACHADO

POSITION: Striker **DOB:** 06/03/1991
COUNTRY: Spain

A fortnight ahead of making their Premier League debut against champions Liverpool, Leeds United confirmed the club-record signing of Spanish international striker Rodrigo from Valencia.

The 29-year-old attacker who can operate as a winger or in a more central striking role agreed a four-year deal with the Whites and looks all set to thrill the Elland Road fans in 2020/21.

There are five Lucas the Kop Kats hiding in the crowd as Leeds fans celebrate winning the First Division title at Loftus Road in 1974. Can you find him?

CLASSIC FANTASTIC

SOCCER SKILLS
DEFENDING

Defending is an art - not as spectacular as swerving a free kick around the wall into the net or floating a crossfield pass into the path of an oncoming wingback - but nevertheless, just as important. Every successful team has a solid defence and can defend as a team.

Defenders must also master the art of defending one on one...

EXERCISE ONE

Two adjacent 10m x 10m grids have two players, X and Y at the opposite ends of the grids. X plays the ball to Y, who is then allowed to attack defender X with the ball. Y's target is to be able to stop the ball, under control, on the opposite end line. Defender X has to try to stop this happening. Y is encouraged to be direct and run at X with the ball.

KEY FACTORS

1. Do not approach the attacker square on. Adopt a sideways stance which enables rapid forward and backwards movement.
2. Do not dive in. Be patient and wait for your opponent to make a mistake. Always be on your toes.
3. Threaten the ball without actually committing to a tackle. Pretending to tackle can often panic the opponent!
4. Tackle when you are sure you will win it!

EXERCISE TWO

Here the game is progressed to a two v two situation when X1 and X2 play as a team against Y1 and Y2.

The same target is used for this game - the players have to stand on the opposite line with the ball, either by dribbling past their opponents or by passing the ball through them.

The same key factors are relevant here with the addition of two more:

5. Covering your defending partner when he is being attacked.
6. Communication between the two defenders is vital.

If a team can get these points of defending right, throughout the side, they will become very difficult to beat.

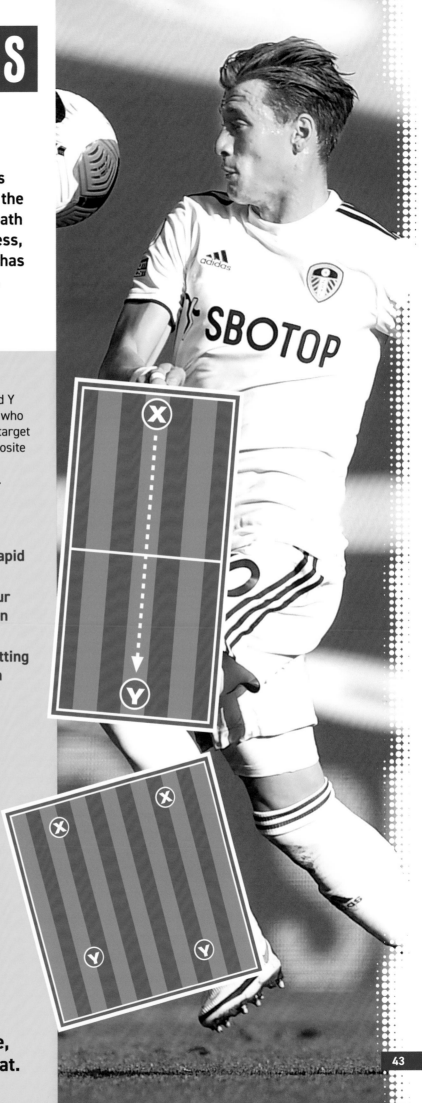

Here are our predictions for the 2020/21 season, see if you agree!

2020/21

PREMIER LEAGUE

OUR PREDICTION FOR PREMIER LEAGUE WINNERS:

LEICESTER CITY

YOUR PREDICTION:

OUR PREDICTION FOR PREMIER LEAGUE RUNNERS-UP:

LIVERPOOL

YOUR PREDICTION:

CHAMPIONSHIP

OUR PREDICTION FOR CHAMPIONSHIP WINNERS:

WATFORD

YOUR PREDICTION:

OUR PREDICTION FOR CHAMPIONSHIP RUNNERS-UP:

SWANSEA CITY

YOUR PREDICTION:

TOP SCORERS

OUR PREDICTION FOR PREMIER LEAGUE TOP SCORER:
PIERRE-EMERICK AUBAMEYANG

YOUR PREDICTION:

OUR PREDICTION FOR CHAMPIONSHIP TOP SCORER:
IVAN TONEY

YOUR PREDICTION:

FA CUP & EFL CUP

OUR PREDICTION FOR FA CUP WINNERS:
LEEDS UNITED

YOUR PREDICTION:

OUR PREDICTION FOR EFL CUP WINNERS:
TOTTENHAM HOTSPUR

YOUR PREDICTION:

PREDICTIONS

PASCUL 21 STRUIJK

POSITION: Defender   **DOB:** 11/08/1999
COUNTRY: Netherlands

Defender Pascul Struijk joined Leeds United from Ajax in January 2018. A left-footed central-defender, who can also operate as a defensive-midfielder, Struijk had to be patient for his first-team chance at Elland Road.

He debuted in December 2019, when the Whites overcame Hull City at home and made five first-team appearances in the club's 2019/20 Championship title-winning campaign. He then made his Premier League debut in the opening day thriller with Liverpool at Anfield.

22 JACK HARRISON

POSITION: Midfielder   **DOB:** 20/11/1996
COUNTRY: England

Having featured in every league game in 2019/20 when Leeds United won the Sky Bet Championship title, the Whites secured winger Jack Harrison's services again for the 2020/21 campaign after he agreed a new season-long loan from Manchester City.

A star performer throughout Marcelo Bielsa's time at Elland Road, Harrison provided eight assists last season and will now be looking to shine on the Premier League stage.

KALVIN 23 PHILLIPS

POSITION: Midfielder **DOB:** 02/12/1995
COUNTRY: England

Local hero Kalvin Phillips has progressed though the Leeds United Academy system and having made his first-team debut back in 2015, he is now closing in on 200 appearances for the club.

An all-action midfielder, Phillips made 37 appearances in last season's title success and struck the only goal of the game to secure a 1-0 Elland Road victory over Birmingham City in October 2019. His club form was rewarded with an England debut against Denmark in the UEFA Nations League in September 2020.

24 LEIF DAVIS

POSITION: Defender **DOB:** 31/12/1999
COUNTRY: England

Something of a lucky charm for Leeds United, young defender Leif Davis became the first player to end on the winning side in each of his first seven league appearances for the club after featuring in the 2-1 win over Blackburn Rovers in November 2019.

Signed from League Two Morecambe in the summer of 2018, Davis has featured regularly for the under-23 side while pushing for first-team action.

47

SOCCER SKILLS
CHEST CONTROL

Controlling the ball quickly and with minimum fuss allows you to get the ball where you want it, so you can pass or shoot. It can be the difference between a good player and a top class player.

EXERCISE ONE

Grab two of your mates to start the exercise. A and C stand 10 yards apart and have a ball each, ready to act as servers.

B works first. B must run towards A who serves the ball for B to control with the chest and pass back to A. B then turns, runs to C and repeats the exercise.

Once B has worked for 30 seconds all the players rotate.

KEY FACTORS

1. Look to control the ball as early as possible.
2. Get in line with the ball.
3. Keep eyes on the ball.
4. Relax the body on impact with the ball to cushion it.

EXERCISE TWO

In this exercise there are five servers positioned around a 15 yard square. At one side of the square there is a goal.

T starts in the middle of the square. S1 serves first, throwing the ball in the air towards T. T must control the ball with the chest and try to shoot past the goalkeeper. As soon as T has shot on goal they must prepare for the next serve from S2.

Once T has received a ball from every server the players rotate positions - the same key factors apply.

Players who can control a ball quickly, putting the ball in a position for a shot or pass, give themselves and their teammates the extra valuable seconds required in today's intense style of play.

Challenge your favourite grown-up and find out which of you is the biggest Premier League brain!

ADULTS

Which other Premier League club has Everton boss Carlo Ancelotti previously been in charge of?

11 ANSWER

Who is the current longest-serving manager in the Premier League?

12 ANSWER

From which then non-league club did Leicester City sign Jamie Vardy?

13 ANSWER

England goalkeeper Jordan Pickford joined Everton from which club?

14 ANSWER

What nationality is Southampton manager Ralph Hasenhuttl?

15 ANSWER

Brighton midfielder Alexis Mac Allister plays international football for which country?

16 ANSWER

Other than Crystal Palace, which other Premier League side has Wilfried Zaha played for?

17 ANSWER

At which club was Jurgen Klopp managing before taking over at Anfield?

18 ANSWER

Which kit manufacturer produces Manchester City's 2020/21 playing strip?

19 ANSWER

What nationality is West Ham 'keeper Lukasz Fabianski?

20 ANSWER

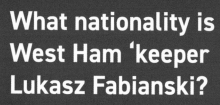

V KIDS

The adults' questions are on the left page and the kids' questions are on the right page.

ANSWERS ON PAGE 62

What is the name of Sheffield United's home stadium?

11

How many teams make up the Premier League?

12

Which was the first club to win the Premier League title?

13 ANSWER

Which Premier League club has the nickname 'the Foxes'?

14

England captain Harry Kane plays his club football for which team?

15 ANSWER

Current Arsenal manager Mikel Arteta is a former Gunners player – true or false?

16 ANSWER

Who is Liverpool's captain?

17 ANSWER

Which London club play their home matches at the London Stadium?

18 ANSWER

How many clubs are relegated from the Premier League each season?

19

What nationality is Manchester City midfielder Kevin De Bruyne?

20

51

BOYS OF 1992

The meteoric rise of Leeds United under the management of Howard Wilkinson reached its pinnacle in 1991/92 when the club were crowned First Division champions.

Wilkinson proved to be a phenomenal success at Elland Road. He led the club back to the top flight in 1989/90 as Second Division champions before overseeing an excellent fourth-place finish in the top flight in 1990/91. The following season, the Whites edged out Manchester United to secure the club's third top-flight title triumph.

Solid in every department, the side boasted an exceptional midfield quartet of skipper Gordon Strachan,

GORDON STRACHAN

In the space of just three seasons, Scotland international midfielder Gordon Strachan captained Leeds United to both the Second and First Division titles as his quality and experience proved invaluable to the team's success.

Despite suffering with an ongoing back complaint, Strachan, who celebrated his 35th birthday in February 1992, proved an inspirational leader and featured in 36 league games in this memorable title-winning campaign.

He scored four league goals including a brace in the 4-0 victory away against Southampton in August 1991. He also netted against Arsenal and Manchester City before hoisting the First Division championship trophy aloft at Elland Road on the final day of the season.

Gary McAllister, David Batty and Gary Speed. England international Steve Hodge was another goalscoring option in midfield, while leading scorer Lee Chapman and striker partner Rod Wallace proved the perfect little and large front two.

Wilkinson's men made a flying start to the season and suffered only one league defeat prior to Christmas. The mid-season signing of Eric Cantona added additional firepower and flair to the team as a two-way battle for the title with arch-rivals Manchester United ensued.

Leeds secured top spot with a game to spare when they finally saw off the challenge of the Red Devils by winning their penultimate game of the season away at Sheffield United. A thrilling 3-2 Yorkshire derby triumph at Bramall Lane was followed by Liverpool defeating Manchester United and the title heading to Elland Road.

A crowd of 32,673 packed into Elland Road for the final game of the season when a Rod Wallace goal earned a 1-0 win over Norwich City. That final win saw Leeds end the season with 82 points and they paraded the First Division trophy in front of their jubilant fans.

TEAM 2020/21

MATEUSZ 43
KLICH

POSITION: Midfielder **DOB:** 13/06/1990
COUNTRY: Poland

Polish international midfielder Mateusz Klich scored six goals in the Whites' 2019/20 Championship title-winning campaign, with his long-range strike against Middlesbrough in November 2019 landing him the Championship Goal of the Month award.

A key figure in the 'Bielsa era' at Leeds, Klich put pen to paper on a new four-and-a-half year contract with the club in late 2019 to the delight of all at Elland Road.

GAETANO 28
BERARDI

POSITION: Defender **DOB:** 21/08/1988
COUNTRY: Switzerland

Gaetano Berardi is a versatile defender who can operate in either full-back berth or in a central-defensive role if called upon. A Swiss international, Berardi joined Leeds back in 2014 from Italian giants Sampdoria.

Sadly, Berardi was injured in the penultimate game of the 2019/20 Championship-winning season, a 3-1 victory against Derby County, but will be looking to regain both full fitness and his place in the team to play his part in the Premier League.

JAMIE 46
SHACKLETON

POSITION: Midfielder **DOB:** 08/10/1999
COUNTRY: England

Academy graduate Jamie Shackleton celebrated Leeds United's promotion-winning season in style by ending the campaign with his first two goals for the club.

The Leeds-born midfielder made 22 Championship appearances in 2019/20 and was on target in the 3-1 win away against Derby County before then netting the club's final goal of an historic season when he added the Whites' fourth goal in their final-day victory over Charlton Athletic. The youngster then agreed a new four-year contract at the club in August 2020.

JARGON BUSTER

Here is a list of footy jargon. All but one of the terms are hidden in the grid... can you work out which is missing?

- All To Play For
- Back Of The Net
- Bags Of Pace
- Big Game Player
- Box-To-Box
- Class Act
- Derby Day
- Dinked In
- Early Doors
- Funny Old Game
- Game Of Two Halves
- Handbags
- Hat-Trick
- Hollywood Pass
- Keep It Tight
- Massive Game
- Midfield General
- Natural Goalscorer
- Row Z
- Worldy

```
A S M Z U C E M A G E V I S S A M
V A W T B X O W A C V T S V Y B N
P O I B Y D I N K E D I N B R Q A
R L Q C J K X Z E F M L F J N E T
O G F W K C I R T T A H C S A Z U
E X B H D A V A P N H X G B J E R
T K A L L T O P L A Y F O R D C A
I R C P M E Q M O L R X G H O A L
F L K D N U R A S T T P K Q C P G
U F O N Z Y D I W O M W Y I B F O
N H F W Z O E S B U N E H L O A L
N J T G O B N O D F F X K A D S S
Y Z H S V R X M A G V O R N I G S
O X E A D C L H H G A E U D Z A C
L B N K Q J L D C J N K A B I B O
D D E R B Y D A Y E E S P A L B R
G W T E U O I P G J I O J G S M E
A C I O K I R D Y U X K T S F A R
M H W V Y B L T B P C H F O R R A
E O P C D E E T G E G Q B L P E N
V G C M I H A F M I E K Y V Z G L
H J B F D W A R T X I D H D C T D
L X D M O A S T A S O L G A T C R
V I A Q K Y I H S O D W J H Y A Q
M P F E Z P R G R G U N F M I S G
Z I N Q E J N S L P I K Z Y S O
D B S E V L A H O W T F O E M A G
A E K T X S L T E M X K W U L L I
S U S N Q L U W E A B V R S P C O
T A Y O R S F I T W Y O T A N B M
B H O L L Y W O O D P A S S U T I
```

MATEUSZ

KLICH

Want to leap like Kiko Casilla, have the strength of Luke Ayling or boast the endurance of Helder Costa? Build up your strength for action with our...

30 DAY

Day 1
Right let's get started! 10 squats, 25 star jumps, 10 sit-ups - all before school!

Day 2
Make your mum a brew before going out to practice your keepy-uppys

Day 3
10 squats
50 star jumps
10 sit-ups

Day 4
How about swapping the crisps in your lunchbox for an apple?

Day 5
Take a one mile ride on your bike

Day 6
75 star jumps
15 sit-ups
15 press-ups

Day 7
Help clean the car before going out to play headers and volleys with your friends

Day 8
75 star jumps
15 sit-ups
15 press-ups
Before and after school now!

Day 9
Walk to school rather than take the bus

Day 10
Head to the swimming pool for a 30-minute swim

Day 11
100 star jumps
20 sit-ups
20 press-ups
Twice a day now, don't forget!

Day 12
Make sure you trade one of your fizzy drinks for a glass of water today

Day 13
Jog to the shop for your mum... before playing any video games!

Day 14
Give a hand around the house before kicking your ball against the wall 500 times

Day 15
Time to increase those exercises!
25 squats
25 sit-ups
25 press-ups
Before and after school!

Day 16
Take a nice paced two-mile jog today

Day 17
25 squats
150 star jumps
25 press-ups
Remember, before and after school

Day 18
Cycle to school rather than rely on the bus or a lift

Day 19
30 squats
150 star jumps
30 press-ups
Twice a day too!

Day 20
Get out and practice those free-kicks, practice makes perfect remember...

Day 21
Get peddling! Time for a two-mile trip on two wheels today

Day 22
Upping the workload now...
40 squats, 40 sit-ups
40 press-ups
Before and after school!

Day 23
Wave goodbye to the chips - ask for a nice salad for lunch today

Day 24
40 squats
40 sit-ups
40 press-ups
Twice a day, don't forget...

Day 25
Time to get pounding the streets - the jogging is up to three miles today

Day 26
45 star jumps
45 sit-ups
45 press-ups

Day 27
Time to swap those sweets and biscuits for some fruit

Day 28
45 star jumps
45 sit-ups
45 press-ups

Day 29
You're getting fitter and fitter now! Keep up the squats and star jumps plus join an after-school sports club - ideally football!

Day 30
Well done - you made it!
50 squats, 50 sit-ups and 50 press-ups!
These are the core ingredients to your success

CHALLENGE
to improve your all-round footy fitness!

ANSWERS

PAGE 16 · ADULTS V KIDS

Adults

1. Conor Coady. 2. Arsenal, Chelsea, Manchester City and Manchester United. 3. Derby County.
4. Roy Hodgson, Crystal Palace. 5. AFC Bournemouth.
6. Sporting Lisbon. 7. Gillingham. 8. Four – Blackburn Rovers, Liverpool, Manchester City and Manchester United. 9. Arsenal. 10. Frank Lampard, Chelsea.

Kids

1. Liverpool. 2. German. 3. Five - Leeds United, Manchester United, Newcastle United, Sheffield United and West Ham United. 4. Wolverhampton Wanderers.
5. Manchester United/Old Trafford. 6. Manchester City.
7. The Toffees. 8. Newcastle United. 9. Brendan Rodgers. 10. Portuguese.

PAGE 20 · WHO ARE YER?

1. Patrick Bamford. 2. Kalvin Phillips.
3. Luke Ayling. 4. Pablo Hernandez.
5. Helder Costa. 6. Jack Harrison.
7. Illan Meslier. 8. Robin Koch.
9. Ian Poveda. 10. Mateusz Klich.

PAGE 40
CLASSIC FANTASTIC ➡

PAGE 50 · ADULTS V KIDS

Adults

11. Chelsea. 12. Sean Dyche, Burnley. 13. Fleetwood Town. 14. Sunderland. 15. Austrian. 16. Argentina.
17. Manchester United. 18. Borussia Dortmund.
19. Puma. 20. Polish.

Kids

11. Bramall Lane. 12. 20 teams. 13. Manchester United.
14. Leicester City. 15. Tottenham Hotspur. 16. True.
17. Jordan Henderson. 18. West Ham United. 19. Three.
20. Belgian.

PAGE 56 · JARGON BUSTER

Big Game Player